uıblróe

ic Libra

ve

INKLE
WEAVING

Lavinia Bradley

WEAVING

A comprehensive manual

ROUTLEDGE & KEGAN PAUL
London, Boston, Melbourne and Henley

First published in 1982
by Routledge & Kegan Paul Ltd
39 Store Street, London WC1E 7DD,
9 Park Street, Boston, Mass. 02108, USA,
296 Beaconsfield Parade, Middle Park,
Melbourne, 3206, Australia, and
Broadway House, Newtown Road,
Henley-on-Thames, Oxon RG9 1EN
Set in Optima by
Rowland Phototypesetting Ltd, Bury St Edmunds, Suffolk
and printed in Great Britain by
St Edmundsbury Press, Bury St Edmunds, Suffolk
© Lavinia Bradley 1982

Library of Congress Cataloging in Publication Data

Bradley, Lavinia.
Inkle weaving.

Bibliography: p.
Includes index.
1. Inkle weaving.   I. Title.
TT848.B68   1982   746.1'4   82-7709

ISBN 0-7100-9086-2   AACR2

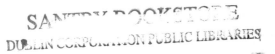

CONTENTS

Preface   vii
Acknowledgments   ix

THE INKLE LOOM   1
What it is   1
Brief history   2

PREPARING TO WEAVE   5
Leashes   5
Warping   6
To warp   7
The warp   9
How to read a warping
   pattern   10

STARTING TO WEAVE   11
Pulling the warp around the
   loom   12
Tension   13
Securing ends   13
Plainweave   15

THE MECHANICS   16
Shaping   16
Tubing   17
Curves   17
Sculptured braids   18
Instant fringes   18
Scallops and loops   18

Buttonholes   19
Slits   19
Cutting up   20

PICK-UPS   21
Simple pick-up   21
Double pick-ups   23
Intensive pick-ups   23
The Peruvian design   26

'KNUBBLING' YOUR KNOTS   29

WRAPPING WARPS   31
Windows   31
Let's go African   33
Necklace   34
Belt   34

LETTERING   35
Warping   35
Floating threads   38

BOLIVIAN PEBBLE WEAVE   40
Summer and winter with the
   Navajo and Home for
   Christmas   40

RAGS   45
Spaced warps   45

Contents

From rags to patches   48

CHRISTMAS TIME   50
Cards by the yard   50
Hanging Christmas trees   51

DYEING FOR A DIAGONAL   55
Exploiting uneven sheds   55

WEFTS   59
Supplementary wefts   59
Insertions   60
Floating wefts   61
Beadwork   64

ALL MANNER OF THINGS   65
Moccasin slippers   65
A log cabin patchwork
   cushion   66

Stuffed bands   66
Woven bands   67
An evening bag   67
Another quick evening
   bag   68
Purse/pencil case   68
Shoulder and shopping bags   69
Furnishings   70
Clothing   70

VALEDICTION   72

APPENDIX: HOW TO MAKE
   YOUR OWN INKLE LOOM   73
Glossary   78
Select bibliography   79
Index   81

PREFACE

This book has been written because of the tremendous interest in inkle weaving, and the lack of information on anything more than its most elementary techniques. My husband, who is a maker of inkle looms, is continually asked by his customers for a comprehensive guide to the craft. There are a few publications giving the basic beginnings, and many good, brief, chapters in books of general weaving, but they all tend to touch on one or two aspects only.

This is a book, therefore, for inkle weavers who so often do not realise the full potential of their loom because there is no comprehensive guide to their craft.

It is also a book for established weavers who have larger looms, to show how an inkle can be a complement to their workshop.

And it is a book for the hundreds of people who would love to weave but have no space, little money, and no one to show them how. It is weaving at its simplest, and yet with expertise it can be as sophisticated as weaving on a 6-shaft loom. A weaver with an inkle loom once said: 'No home should be without one.' I hope this book will convince you, for it is for all sorts of people and conditions.

Lavinia Bradley

ACKNOWLEDGMENTS

I should like to thank my kind photographers – John Hitchens for the cover print, Mrs Audrey Fawley for the historic photograph of Mary Atwater, and Rosalind Hitchens, Kay Kettle and Toby Harvey, and my sons Caleb and Jason.

Also Quin Farmer and Marianne Meadows, and all my friends and students who encouraged me to write the book.

THE INKLE LOOM

WHAT IT IS

'Inkle' is the Old English word for a linen band or drawstring, hence an inkle loom is a loom on which these were made. The word has been in the language in one form or another for over 400 years (see Glossary), but was used in its modern spelling by Shakespeare in *The Winter's Tale* (see Glossary).

Today with zips and fasteners, we forget how much people once had to rely on bands, not only for carrying, bundling, belting and trimming, but simply for keeping their clothing up. Inkles were very necessary.

The loom is also sometimes referred to as a Scottish Braid Loom, but I do not like this name at all as it gives the impression that it is limited to making only braids – a belief that is very common, but which I hope to dispel.

An inkle loom differs from other looms in that it has a continuous warp, which is wound directly onto the loom without the need for any separate warping, and the sheds for weaving are made by taking alternate threads over a peg and pulling them down with a leash, without any need to thread a reed or heddles.

Its other feature is a tension adjuster to give control of the warp tension throughout the work.

There are various models of inkles, but they must all fulfil these three basic features:

- a continuous warp;
- a simple leash method to make sheds; and
- a device for controlling warp tension.

It is also unique in that it is the only loom to have uneven sheds, which we shall exploit later in this book.

1

BRIEF HISTORY

The Old English inkle loom was a floor model, with a sliding peg for its tension adjuster, and set-in leashes

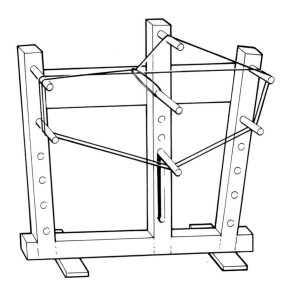

Old English floor model

From this developed a model with rollers at either end, as in a conventional loom, to give greater lengths, but, although so called, it is not strictly speaking an inkle loom, since the warp is not continuous

Roughly eighty years ago, E. E. Gilmore, a Californian, adapted the old floor inkle loom to a table model, which was less bulky, mobile, and much more comfortable to use. It is from this basic design that today's inkle looms have sprung.

Today's loom has greatly refined the Gilmore model. It no longer has a sliding tension peg, but a cam-type tension adjuster, which is sited near the working sheds and allows a much finer control and is easier to use. The leashes are warped and tied on the loom itself at will, and the whole can be dismounted for storage.

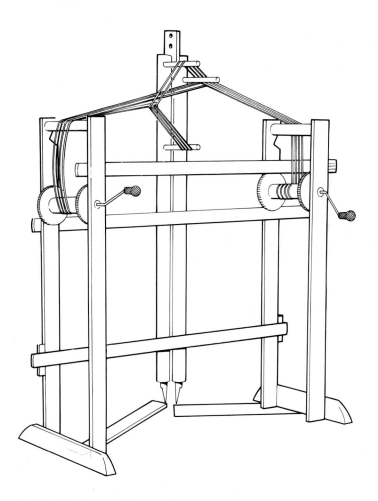

Model with rollers and foot pedals

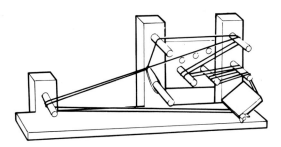

The Gilmore table model

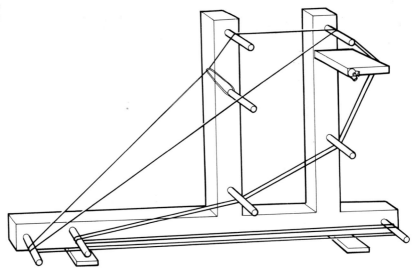

Today's dismountable, lightweight model

PREPARING TO WEAVE

The basis of all weaving is darning – vertical threads called **the warp** must be crossed with horizontal threads running in and out called **the weft**.

←— Warp

←— Warp with weft

The prospect of darning a whole fabric being too laborious to entertain, looms were invented. Their function is to manipulate the long, or warp, threads in such a way that the action of the darning thread, or weft, can be sent across in one movement instead of having to go in and out each warp thread separately, and to achieve this looms must be threaded up through heddles and a reed, which is the most tedious and exacting part of weaving. It is hard on your eyes and your temper, and any mistake will multiply throughout your work.

However, an inkle loom needs no such threading. You simply wind your yarn around a series of pegs, according to the length required, and to make your sheds possible (as the divisions for your in and out movements are called) you pull down every alternate thread taken over a top peg with a leash.

LEASHES

Leashes are simply loops which anchor threads to the leash pegs. They should be strong and smooth – strong because you will use them again and again, and smooth so that you can pull your work through them as you progress around your loom. Cotton, rayon or linen is suitable. Wool is not, since its hairy fibres cling.

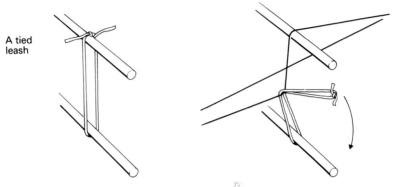

A tied leash

Showing how the leash, anchored on the leash peg, pulls down the thread going over the top peg and holds it down

To tie your leashes, wind your yarn around the two pegs astride the tension adjuster. You will need half as many leashes as threads. Cut the threads and you will have uniform lengths to tie on the next two pegs with a reef knot. In some books this is called a square knot. The important thing is that it will not slip, for uneven leashes will give you an uneven shed.

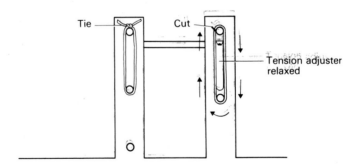

Tie

Cut

Tension adjuster relaxed

WARPING

We are now ready to begin. The Old English inkle bands were woven in linen, and indeed *Webster's Dictionary* specifies linen as the material for inkle weaving, but modern weavers use anything from finest silks to 6 ply wools. As in any work, different materials require different handling – for instance wool will stretch, but there is no elasticity in linen or silk, so that the tension adjuster on the loom needs to be used differently. Remembering always that it is the warp that takes the strain, a wide variety of materials can be used. We shall deal in different materials as we progress, but let us start with wool, since it is the best humoured.

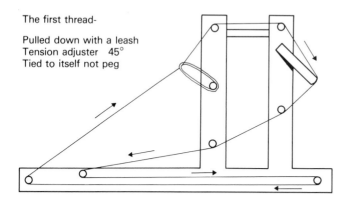

The first thread-

Pulled down with a leash
Tension adjuster   45°
Tied to itself not peg

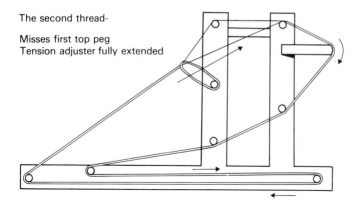

The second thread-

Misses first top peg
Tension adjuster fully extended

TO WARP

Before you start, **position your tension adjuster at 45°**. This is to ensure that the first (and last) threads are tighter than the body of the work, which is necessary to get a firm selvedge. If you do NOT use your tension adjuster in this way, when you take the work from the loom, and the tension is reduced, you will have edges that look like ocean waves.

7

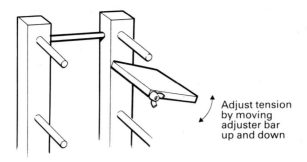

Adjust tension
by moving
adjuster bar
up and down

Select the path around the pegs for the length you require. There are a great many variations. In the diagram I show you the longest (9ft (2.77m) on a Bradley loom).

Run your yarn along the pegs and leaving a tail tie it firmly **on to it-self**. It's a common fault to tie it to the back peg, when of course it is impossible to pull the work around the loom.

Take a leash, anchor it on the leash peg, then slip it over your thread and pull it down as shown.

Now extend your tension adjuster to its maximum.

Now wind the same journey, missing the top peg. This is called the open shed and needs no leash.

You repeat this winding of threads, alternately over the top peg with a leash and an open thread without one, until you come to the last thread, preferably a leash thread. Here you once again release the tension adjuster and tie the thread firmly on to itself, and then the two tails of yarn, from the start and the finish, together.

You have now made your first warp – the most difficult and least interesting thing you ever do on your inkle loom.

Some people put on a tight warp, and some a loose one. It is like knitting, you will have your own style, and it doesn't matter how you do it provided you are **consistent**. You must not have loose threads and then tight ones, or vice versa; all threads must be the same tension, and this is a knack that comes automatically with practice.

If you are interrupted in the middle of warping, twist your thread around a peg before you get up and leave it to keep the tension. If you just let go, the slack will run back into the warp you have already made, and you will have to start again.

You do the same thing when you want to tie in different colours. Once they are started, you twist them around each other to keep in the tension as you change from one to another. I have seen weavers cut and tie their yarn every time they change the colour, which uses up a great deal of thread and time, and looks very unsightly on the loom.

Twisting your threads not only saves yarn and time, and is correct in making your warp **continuous**, but also serves to show how even you are making your tension. The twists should be in a neat straight line. If you have let a thread go loose, the twist will be above its fellows — too tight, it will be below.

THE WARP

Inkle weaving is warp-faced. You must pull your weft tight enough to hide it. This makes a very strong dense weave, and is the reverse of tapestry weaving, where you only see the weft.

Therefore, in your first plain inkle weave, your pattern will be in the colours and types of thread you have put into your warp. You will soon see there is a wide variety in these patterns according to how you tie in different colours when you make the warp. Also in the thicknesses and types of yarn you use and mix. Very simply, here are a few pointers to start with:

- **One coloured thread** in a background will give you a spot. This is because, as in darning, first you see the coloured thread, and then you don't, as it goes through one shed and then the next. It can be arranged as a pin stripe, or staggered as a polka dot pattern, or used in a design of its own.

- **Two coloured threads** side by side will give you a line.

- **Three coloured threads** side by side will give you a line with a bump in it, which can look like a cable.

- **Two different colours** wound on alternately will give you horizontal bars of the two colours. These you twist around each other at the start of each journey around the loom.

- **Three**, or **five**, or **seven** different colours laid one after another will give you a tweed effect. These, too, must be twisted, and the knack is to lay the last colour along the side of the loom farthest from you, taking the nearest for the next warp, so the colours are always moving towards you. This may sound rather pedantic, but when you are using five or more colours, it can become confusing if you have no system. In this way, the newest thread nearest you automatically twists around the others lying in order along the base of the loom, and you will have no trouble.

So that you can play with some designs, and also record your own, this is how you read an inkle pattern.

HOW TO READ A WARPING PATTERN

Warping patterns are written with an upper line for the leash threads, over a lower line for the open threads. Thus alternate red and blue threads to make horizontal bars in the weave, with the red threads over the top peg and pulled down with leashes, and the blue ones open, looks like this:

Leash →	R	R	R	R	R	R
Open →		B	B	B	B	B	B

A simple 3-coloured tweed is:

X	—	O	X	—	O	X	—
	O	X	—	O	X	—	O

A chain is:

X	X	X	O	O	X	X	X
	X	X	O	X	O	X	X

Put another colour in the centre of your chain, beat it down extra hard, and it becomes a flower.

X	X	X	O	O	X	X			
	X	X	O	—	O	X			

This is a chequerboard:

X	X	X	O	O	O	X	X	X	O	O	O			
O	O	O	X	X	X	O	O	O	X	X	X			

This is called the 'come-on' pattern, which will explain itself. It can go on for ever as long as you supply the next colour.

X	X	X	X	X	X	O	O	O	O	O	+	+	+	+		etc
	X	X	O	O	O	O	O	+	+	+	+	+	—	—	—

Of course, thick and thin threads will make a pattern in the weave, and as you progress you will be able to create more sophisticated colour patterns, and plain textures, by transferring threads from one shed to another. But let us now start to weave.

STARTING TO WEAVE

First, sit comfortably. Weaving is rhythmic and relaxing, and with an inkle loom you can select your favourite chair, prop the far feet of the loom on a table and rest it in your lap. You can take it out into the garden if you can find a low wall or fence to rest the far feet upon.

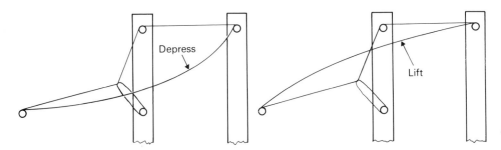

Shed 1 (leash threads on top)　　　　　　Shed 2 (open threads on top)

BACKSTOP   Before you actually start to weave, uplift the threads immediately behind the leashes (see Shed 2 above) and slip a small piece of stick or card – a child's flat ice-lolly stick is perfect – into the shed you have made, in front of the leashes and press it back as far as it will go against the back peg. This is simply to give you something to beat against when you begin to weave.

WEFT   Wind your weft onto your flat wooden shuttle. This will be passed from side to side through the two sheds you make by alternately uplifting, or depressing, the open warp threads immediately behind the leashes (see sheds 1 and 2).

   As inkle weaving is warp-faced, this weft will be invisible save at the edges of your work as it turns the corner to enter the next shed. If it is the same colour as the outer threads of the work, it will not show. If it is a different colour, it will be a little spot up the sides of your braid.

TO WEAVE   Uplifting, or depressing the open threads immediately behind the leashes to make your sheds to take the shuttle may be done with your hand or a small stick. I find a short, flat, stick quick and sure and I press it down, or up with my thumb.

With your right hand, or stick in right hand, depress the threads behind the leashes, and enter your shuttle of yarn from the left across the warp, leaving a tail of yarn as long as the breadth of the work. Beat it down with the edge of your shuttle, or small stick, and then pull it until the loop of weft has disappeared. The most common fault of inkle weaver beginners is loose weft loops at the edges of their braids, and this is generally because they beat the yarn down and fail to pull in that little fullness made by pressing the yarn flat in the shed.

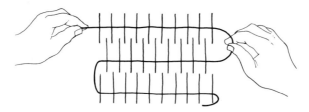

Pulling the weft after beating it down,
to take up any slack

Again with the right hand, uplift the open threads and in the same manner as before send the weft back across the warp to the left, and beat it down, being careful to tighten the weft.

As you repeat these two actions, the worked warp will speedily climb upwards towards the leashes, and you will need to pull it around the loom to give yourself more room to advance.

PULLING THE WARP AROUND THE LOOM

Lift the open threads – this gives less resistance when you pull as they are free of leashes.

Relax the tension adjuster and pull the open threads towards you. This will move the whole warp along the frame. You may find the fibres of a woollen warp will cling to the leashes, and you can only pull as far as the leashes will lean. To overcome this, you pull in a series of little

12

jerks to the limit of the leashes, pushing them up and pulling again until you have enough warp to continue with. In cotton, linen, or man-made fibres there is no cling and the whole work will slip through the leashes easily.

Tighten the tension adjuster and begin again.

TENSION

As the weft works its way in and out, it takes up a fractional amount of the warp, so that the work tightens as it proceeds. If you are using wool, which has elasticity, this is usually so slight that you only notice when you come to match patterns in the making-up of the braid – the motif is a little longer at the end of the warp than it was at the beginning. This is easily overcome by compensating with the tension adjuster, letting it out as you need.

SECURING ENDS

At the beginning of this chapter, I emphasised that you should leave a tail of weft as long as the breadth of the warp. This is so that in your second shed you can take this end back into the warp with the next weft throw, so that the second shed of the weave has a double weft – its own and the tail of the beginning. This locks the end securely into the weave, and will prevent fraying when the work is cut off.

The same happens in the last-but-one weft throw when you reach the other end. Slip a needle, or crochet hook into the last up-shed along with the regular weft. Return on the down-shed, and pull the end through under itself with the needle or hook. Change the shed again and cut the work off. **On no account ever try to darn ends in!**

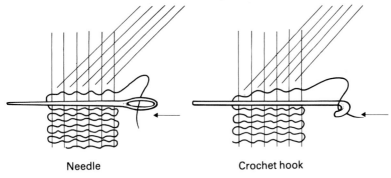

Needle   Crochet hook

The coat, mentioned on page 70, woven in wool in plain-weave, and modelled, by Rosalind Hitchens of Graffham.

PLAINWEAVE

You can now weave a plain inkle strip. Don't let the word 'plain' lead you to undervalue it. I have met inkle weavers who have made a great variety of things with enormous joy who have never ventured further. They have had fun with the colours of their warps, often using imaginative materials, thick and thin, and both together, to create pleasing effects. A shiny thread, or a bouclé strand, in amongst a matt weave can be attractive, and the scope from a fine Sylko (50 threads to ½ inch (12mm)) to a 6 ply rug wool will take you from weaving ribbon to heavy carpet weights. You can experiment with cottons, rayons, linens and jute, string and cord, but above all with every weight and variety of wool. You can double warp threads here and there – twisting two different coloured warp threads as you warp them. The fun you can gain from plainweave is ahead in your experience, and can be vast.

15

THE MECHANICS

Before we go on to more interesting things, one more word on the mechanics. You can shape your weaving, just as you shape knitting when you increase or decrease. You can, of course, do a lot more with it besides, such as make tubes, or sculptured forms, curved braids and so on. These things are useful to know, so that when you are proficient at various weaves, you can make them up into useful things. Eventually one runs out of walls, however delightful wall-hangings can be. You can also have a surfeit of cushions and bags.

SHAPING

A fully fashioned shaping to weaving is achieved by cutting out or tying in threads. The obvious example is a tie, but a waistcoat armhole uses the same treatment on one side instead of both.

There is a clumsy way of narrowing the braid for the tie neck by lessening the tension and pulling the weft tighter, but this makes a bulky, thick, narrowed section with an altered look to the weave. You must cut out your threads for an expert effect.

First study your pattern, if there is one. You take two threads **inside** the braid (not on the edge) that balance. That is, if you cut a thread 9 threads inside the border on one side, take the corresponding thread 9 threads inside the other border. If you are cutting one thread at a time, take the neighbouring one next so that you eliminate a pair, leash and open, and don't leave two leash threads, or two open threads, beside each other, which would alter the weave. Bear in mind that you are making a warp-faced weave, and where you cut out threads the weft will show unless you draw it in tight enough to close the gap. This narrows the braid.

Cut the threads 2 or 3 in. (50 or 75 mm) higher than your weaving, and let the end fall forward over your work, taking the long end around the top of the loom so it is there if you want to tie it in again. The next weft throw will lock in the cut end, so there is never any need to darn it in. When the work is ended, you simply shave it off.

The same applies to tying threads in. Put them in as if you were making a new warp, with the bare thread lying across the section already woven, until you are ready to take braid from the loom and chop the thread away. This is how you re-make broken threads.

It is also how you can colour change within the warp, but that comes later.

TUBING

Tubing is another form of shaping very easily achieved. If done tightly on a few warps, it will make you piping for cushions and upholstery. If done more loosely on a wider strip, it makes excellent handles for bags, and done in string will give you dog leads and collars.

The trick is to lessen tension and weave in the normal way but come in from the same side each time, pulling the yarn tight behind the braid each time.

Bolivians like to edge their cloth with such tubes, they make strong straps for bundling, and I particularly like them when you start with a few inches of plain weave and then tube it until you have the depth of handle you need, and widen it out again at the end for bags. This method, besides being neat and strong and comfortable (it doesn't cut your hand when you carry it) is much more economical in yarn than the usual twisted cords.

CURVES

Curves for necklines and such can be achieved by warping shirring elastic (round elastic) on the side of your warp that will be the inside of the curve. When you take the braid from the loom, and tension is relaxed, the elastic will contract and pull its edge into a curve.

SCULPTURED BRAIDS

Sculptured braids is the rather grand name for another trick much loved by art students, but could have its uses for the average weaver bent on articles that need firm shaping. Here you incorporate fine florist's wire into the braid, which is pliable enough to be manipulated and fine enough to be invisible in the wool. When the braid is taken off the loom, it can be bent into shapes and will hold its form.

INSTANT FRINGES

Instant fringes are another trick. These are useful for pelmets, or edgings of various sorts. Space your warp so that there is a gap in the middle. Take three shuttles, and with the first shuttle weave right across the gap and all throughout the braid. With a finer thread on each of the other shuttles, use one at the left edge, and the other on the right. This can be done on each throw of the main weft, or you can do it every second throw, together or staggered. There is a variety of ways to choose, but the principle is the same. When the braid is finished, you cut up the middle through the plain wefts to form your fringes on either side, and the additional thin wefts on each side will stop the fringed halves from fraying.

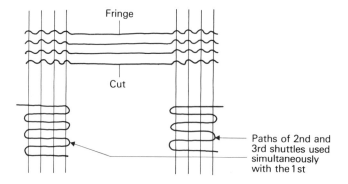

SCALLOPS AND LOOPS

Scallops and loops for edgings of lampshades and such can be made by looping the weft around a pencil as well as the outside warp thread as you turn to re-enter a shed — evenly or staggered. This can be very effective done in silks or heavy cotton, and will save you a great deal of money in trimmings.

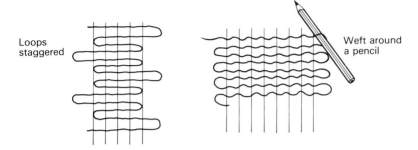

Loops staggered

Weft around a pencil

BUTTONHOLES

Buttonholes are neatly executed vertically, and nothing looks nicer on a hand-knitted cardigan than a narrow woven edging with buttonholes woven in. It is much firmer than a knitted one.

Use two wefts, coming in from each side at the same time, so that they cross in the sheds. This also makes a neater edging, since the weft loops are opposite each other all the way up, instead of staggered.

When you reach the place for your buttonhole, take the wefts to meet in the middle but not cross, change the shed and take them out again. Continue weaving each one individually on its own side until the slit is long enough, and then throw them right across again to close the hole.

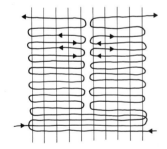

SLITS

Slits can be made as long or, as in buttonholes, as short as you wish, and these can sometimes be very effective in wall-hangings, and useful in places where you want to thread something through, like a belt.

CUTTING UP

When you come to make up your work into articles, a quick trick to eliminate finishing off and restarting ends in the middle of the braids is to stick a piece of Sellotape across them and cut through its centre. This will stop any fraying until you come to sew, and saves beginnings and endings in the work.

PICK-UPS

In plainweave, the pattern of your braid lies entirely in the warp – its colours and materials. Once put upon the loom, there is no further development. However, if you lift threads from one shed to another, you open the door to a new and limitless concept of design.

One of the great advantages of inkle weaving is that every thread is within reach of your fingers – you can hold them all in your hand and manipulate each one at will. This can lead to the most sophisticated weaving.

If you have ever seen a picture of Bolivian weavers at work – who create the most intricate designs, and draw scenes of animals and people with their threads – you will see that however broad their warp may be, they only work it in strips narrow enough to fit an inkle loom. The reason is they need to manipulate each thread individually, and this can only be done if you can reach each one within the grasp of your hand. This you can do on your inkle loom, so let us proceed to the first steps of a **simple pick-up**.

SIMPLE PICK-UP

If this technique is pursued on a plain coloured warp, you will have the pattern stand out in an embossed effect, which can give lovely textures. However, for purposes of learning, it is easier to see what you are doing if you use two colours, green and white.

WARPING   With a border of 6 white threads on each side, warp alternate white and green threads, starting with a white leash, until you have 21 green open threads against the far 6 white border threads.

Weave a few throws of white weft, and you will have white and green

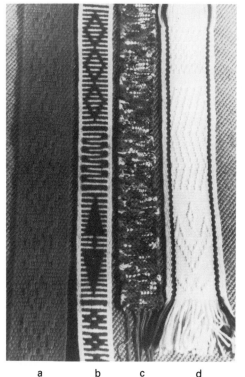

| a | b | c | d | Double pick-up |

PICK-UPS
a and d in self colour for texture
b in colour
c plain rag weave (see Rags, p. 45)

horizontal bars within a white border. We shall now make first a green pattern on these stripes, and then a white one. For a start, let us make a diamond. This is done by a **simple pick-up**.

Make your down-shed. If you part the middle two leashes, you will see the green thread lying depressed between them. Lift it up into the white threads, and throw your weft across.

Change the shed and return the weft.

On the next down-shed, lift two green threads either side of the one you lifted last time, and throw the weft across.

Change the shed and return the weft.

Continue like this, lifting two threads each side of the ones previously lifted on the down-shed, returning the weft on the up-shed plain, until you have 4 double pairs of uplifted threads each side of the middle green one. This will be two green threads to go to the border.

To start to close the diamond, you now uplift two green threads

22

progressively further inwards towards the middle green thread, which will complete the diamond.

Experiment with different shapes – crosses, chevrons, diagonals, etc. until you are used to expressing yourself in green on white.

Now try white on green. This is exactly the same thing, only instead of lifting green threads up on the down-shed, you lift the white ones up into the green on the up-shed, and lock them in with a plain throw on the down-shed. Try a few diamonds and crosses in white.

DOUBLE PICK-UPS

Having now patterned green on white, and white on green, combine the two together. This means that you sacrifice the plain locking returning row, because on the down-shed you are picking up green threads, and on the up-shed you are lifting white ones.

An easy first exercise is to outline a green diamond with a white one immediately inside it. However, the white diamond cannot begin with one thread. The green one begins with one thread, but the white one inside it must start with two.

This pick-up also looks good in self colour. Try lifting every 4th thread on the down-shed, and come back plain. Then lift every 4th thread, starting 2 threads in, on the next down-shed, and come back plain. Repeat these two rows several times, and you have a basket-type weave.

Try this one in colours. If you do first an inch picking up greens, and then switch to an inch picking up whites, you have little windows of green looking into white, and vice versa.

INTENSIVE PICK-UPS

Now we are entering the realm of colour changes, which is exciting weaving. Up to now your pick-ups have been largely outlines, or outlines within outlines. Now we shall fill the outlines in to get solid blocks of colour.

Again we use the same green and white bars warp, but this time we are going to make a solid diamond.

On the down-shed, lift the centre green thread as before, and return the weft on the plain up-shed.

Intensive pick-up in
three colours

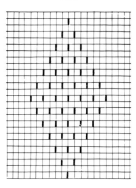

INTENSIVE PICK-UP   SIMPLE PICK-UP

Next down-shed lift the two threads either side of the middle thread, and return on the plain up-shed.

This down-shed, lift the middle thread again with the two on either side of it, and return on the plain up-shed.

Next row, lift the two either side of the middle thread and the two threads either side of them, returning plain.

Continue in this manner adding threads on each side to the threads you lifted before, and you will have a solid green shape.

If at the same time you were also to lift the white threads where the green and white bars are – that is on either side of the solid diamond – you would have a solid green diamond on a solid white background.

Now change the colours over, and lift a solid white diamond on a solid green ground.

You can change only two colours, because you have only warped two colours, so now warp three colours and get **three colour** changes.

THREE COLOURS   Warp 11 alternate threads of yellow and blue (yellow being the leash threads), then change the blue for red for 21 threads, and end with 11 blue and yellow. All the leash threads will be yellow.

You can now have a completely yellow warp by picking up the yellow threads, as in the solid diamond. You can have two blue half-diamonds on either side of a red diamond on a yellow ground. You can switch to yellow half diamonds either side a large yellow diamond on blue and red grounds. You can have blue and yellow, and red and yellow, striped diamonds outlined in blue and red on yellow grounds, or outlined in yellow on blue and red grounds. You can now forget all about diamonds and introduce different shapes in any of the three colours. Once you start to experiment it is fascinating to find how many varying combinations can be made, and you will be ready to try a Peruvian design in **four** colours.

THE PERUVIAN DESIGN

This may be worked in four colours doing the **intensive pick-up**.

A word of caution before you begin. Use a finer weft than the warp, and beat the work down hard. Designs tend to elongate themselves when worked, and this will help. Naturally, this weft will have to be the same colour as the border, so it will be invisible.

For the warp, I would suggest a dark red border, with a dark red and maize colour centre (these being alternate threads) sandwiched between alternate threads of green and a strong blue – your **four colours**.

These two designs joined and edged by plain braids, or lightly striped ones in the four colours, would be splendid for a child's room. Alternatively, in black, beige, grey and white, it becomes suitably masculine for a husband. The choice of colours effectively change the character of the design.

← 42 Leashes →

A Peruvian design

The rubbish rug
  No thread is longer than 10 inches, having been taken from a weaver's waste-
basket and knotted

'KNUBBLING' YOUR KNOTS

This is something you can only do on an inkle loom. It is very **profitable**, making something out of nothing. It **liberates you from geometric designs** based on the right angle of warp to weft, and is a very good reason why conventional weavers should supplement their equipment with an inkle loom.

In every weaver's workshop there is inevitably waste – the short ends left when a piece of work is cut down from the loom, and those small left-overs that are too short or too few to do anything with. This applies also to knitters with their oddments of wool. There are also temptingly inexpensive bundles of wool that can be bought from carpet factories called 'thrums'. All your discarded short ends of yarn can be used on your inkle.

You can do it only on an inkle loom because a knotted warp cannot pass through a reed or rigid heddle of a conventional loom. You also need a very efficient tension adjuster to negotiate your knots, for that's what it's all about – the forbidden feature of every warp – **knots** – which you are going to 'knubble'.

Take two different coloured lengths of wool of about 1½–2 ft (450–600mm) and, laying the two ends together, knot them by taking them around your finger and pulling the ends up through the loop so made, being generous with the ends so that they stick up 1½–2 in. (37–50mm) in the centre of your joined lengths.

Repeat the process, joining more and more lengths to a growing end, varying the colour at each knot, until you have enough yarn to string your loom. Should you have more of one colour than another, repeat that colour more often than any other to use it up, but seldom more than every other knot in order to get the maximum colour changes.

When your loom is strung with this multi-coloured knotted yarn, it will have little 'rabbit-ears' sticking up along the warp in unexpected places, marking the knots, where each thread will change its colour as it winds its way along the loom.

As soon as you begin to make your sheds for weaving, you know why knots in a warp are frowned upon, because, of course, the ends entwine themselves around the other warp threads and stick. To minimise this difficulty, work right up by the leashes, so you will have as few knots as possible to deal with. The length of a leash from the leashes is a good distance. Where the ends stick, just part the threads and pull the ends down towards you. This creates 3 threads to the warp immediately below the knot instead of one, which when woven in will give you your 'knubble' that culminates in the knot itself, out of which a new colour comes.

Thus the individual threads of the woven warp are forever thickening into a blob and changing colour at random places all over the braid.

You will find that when you want to pull the work around the loom, the knots will stick at the leashes, so here you must relax your tension adjuster and help the leashes over the knots with your fingers. I recommend pulling the braid only the length of the leashes each time, which means more relaxing tension and pulling in small doses, but less obstruction from your knots in making the sheds.

It is a change from the straight stripes of so many inkle braids to have this ever-changing colour flow married to the texture, which is not unlike using an exaggerated gimp yarn.

However, although your lines are broken and changing, they do all flow the same way up the work, and I also found it effective to make my weft a solid colour throughout and float a weft thread across diagonally up the work to give the pattern an extra cohesion. If your warp is 50 threads (25 leashes), you float your weft over the 2nd warp thread on the first weft throw, lock it in on the second, float the 3rd warp thread on the 3rd throw, lock it in on the next, float over the 4th warp thread on the 5th throw, and so on for 50. When you reach the far side, you begin again, so that the varied coloured braid is made one by solid-coloured diagonals running across the upward flow of colours. If several braids are done like this and joined to make a rug, the result has no reminder that it has been made up from odds and ends, but presents an original and distinctive face.

WRAPPING WARPS

I always feel like announcing my wrapped warp lesson with 'Let's go African', since there is an African look to wrapped warp belts and chokers and jewellery. It can also have a medieval flavour, as it was done then too. And today I have students wearing waistcoats and tabards decorated with multicoloured wrapped warp windows.

WINDOWS

To introduce this technique, you must start by making plain windows in your warp that you will shape and wrap in various ways with dramatic effect. You must use **two wefts**, each one coming in from a different side and crossing each other in the shed.

(There are weavers who always use two shuttles like this, so that when they come to join their strips the weft end loops are opposite each other instead of staggered. I think it is a waste of time, unless for some special purpose.)

To make your first window, choose its position in the warp — take the centre as a start — and weave each weft individually from its own side to the edge of the window and back again, leaving the warp raw in between. Continue until you have the depth of window you need, then throw both wefts right across, as before, to close the window. This can be done square, or in steps, or whatever shape you select for the window outline. This makes the window, and it can be in different shapes and sizes and in different positions, left, right and centre, in your work.

Now to wrap the raw warps that are the window centre. To get the most dramatic effect, use coloured silk or cotton for wrapping a wool warp. Linen or metallic thread is also very effective. However, wool will do.

Wrapping
warps

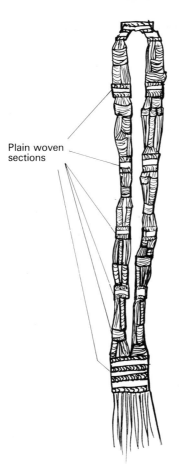

Plain woven
sections

African-style wrapped warp necklet

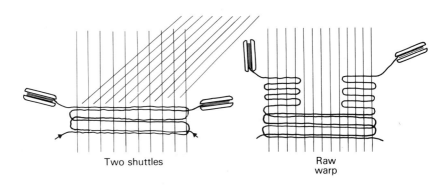

Two shuttles

Raw
warp

In your last double weft throw before making the window, introduce your wrapping thread, whatever it may be, from the right edge of the braid to the left side of the window. When the weft weaving up the sides is completed, it is then waiting to start the wrapping.

With a needle, wind it closely around two (or three or four or five) warp threads, depending on how thick you want the bars of your window, up to the top and then down the next group. Catch the thread into the weave at the base and proceed up another bar and down again until you have enough.

To finish it off, if you are at the window top, the wrapping thread can be run into the weft throw that closes the window. If you are at the bottom, run it into the last bar.

According to the shape of your window, you can imitate prison bars, or church windows, long slits or little peepholes.

According to how you wrap your threads, you can make plain, straight, columns for bars, or you can interlace them into 'fancy ironwork', shapes, initials, etc. The variety is endless.

Woven and wrapped in a plain linen, these windows make a dramatic room divider or wall hanging.

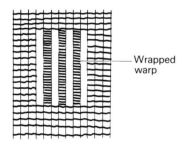
Wrapped warp

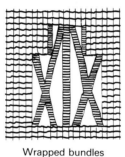
Wrapped bundles caught together

Shaped window

LET'S GO AFRICAN

A window in your weave is a way of decorating solid weaving. Now try experimenting with wrapping warps as an exercise in its own right, and the traditional weave as the decoration in the wrapping. This is the African flavour.

For this, I recommend a dark and light cotton thread. This is because the colour changes after the woven sections play an important part, so need to be distinctive. Here I will give instructions in brown and white.

Start stringing with a solid brown border of 9 threads, with a centre of 20 white threads alternating with 20 brown threads. Thus when you start to weave you will have horizontal brown and white stripes in a brown border. Weave with two shuttles of white, coming in from opposite sides on each throw and crossing in the shed.

After an inch or so, divide the band, using one shuttle to each half, and begin. From here on, you treat each half individually, wrapping at random small groups of threads, leaving raw warp here and there. After 1½ in. (47mm) or so of changing wraps, weave four throws of conventional weave before you begin to wrap again. As your weft, and hence wrapping, is white, the greatest effect is obtained by ending each woven section with the brown shed showing uppermost, as your raw unwrapped threads will then show dark against the white wrappings.

Alternatively, you can occasionally throw an extra weft in the weaving section, and this will change your warp colour to white.

NECKLACE

You will find you can create a startling varied African-style necklet. You continue until the slit between the two sections is long enough to go over your head as a necklace before you join them once again by running the wefts right across as at the start, gathering the braid into a tassel for a pendant.

BELT

Make another braid with 3 in. (75mm) of plain weaving and a matchstick woven into the weft before you divide into 4 divisions for wrapping. After 3 in. (75mm) unite them again with another matchstick hidden in the weft, and weave for 3 in. (75mm) plain. Continue dividing and coming together once more in 3 in. (75mm) sections, with matchsticks before and after each division. This stiffens the braid when it is off the loom, and gives you an intriguing belt.

LETTERING

This seems to be my most popular lesson – perhaps because it is so surprisingly easy to do on an inkle loom **free fingering**. (I stress the **free fingering**, since I have seen it done with six different groups of leashes in a complicated fashion I have never found at all necessary.) I think it may be that it confers a certain expertise on the doer, and undoubtedly it has a useful and attractive end product.

The obvious result is **personalised bookmarks**. Another popular item is named belts for children. I made a belt with 'RUPERT RUPERT RUPERT' all around it, and when Rupert went to school his teacher rang me up and asked if I'd make named belts for all the class, as it was such a help in getting the children interested in their names and letters.

I have also enjoyed weaving lettered samplers with verses, sometimes prayers, for delighted friends. I sent a rhyme to an American weaver, who wrote back – 'It will be an heirloom!' On the strength of that alone, let me explain how it is done.

Bookmarks and belts and samplers are all fairly fine work. This is not always necessary. I have put verse into the borders of rugs in coarse carpet wools with great effect, and I would suggest for a first time you, too, string your loom with wool of a weight you can easily see and pull about.

WARPING

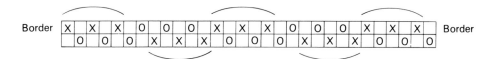

35

Sampler and bookmarkers

This is done with a chequerboard of 30 working threads (15 leashes) within the borders of your background. The x's are the colour the letters will be.

A sampler has a plain background. A bookmark can have a decorative edge, and if part of this edging is a horizontal couple of threads it will not only serve as a decoration but also as a guide to your tension in weaving, and you will be able to count by the bars how many weft throws you have made in the spaces between letters and words, which can sometimes be hard to see.

When you begin to weave, your braid will have a chequerboard pattern running up the working area.

Before starting, notice that your threads are warped in groups of 3 colourwise, and every thread has a partner of the contrasting colour. The first 3 dark leash threads have 3 light open threads beside them, as the light leash threads have dark open threads beside them. It is by exchanging these colour groups of 3 that you form your letters and it is imperative that one colour is always exchanged for another. That is to say, for every dark thread pulled up a light one must go down, and vice versa. Throughout you will be exchanging groups of colour. We must also consider the letters themselves. On this threading, you will have plain, square letters. (If you wanted taller ones, you could arrange groups of 4 threads instead of 3, etc.) Here we begin with the simplest to make and the clearest to read.

Your *letters* will lie on their sides up the braid, so you weave the words as you would write them along a line.

Most of your letters will take 3 throws to make, and here it helps to have squared paper. A, C, E, F, H, L, O, P, S, T and U are all three throw letters, thus:

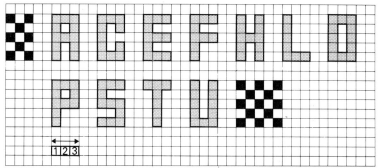

The 3H throw letters

However, letters with diagonals in them take more, as K, M, N, R, V, W, X and Z, so:

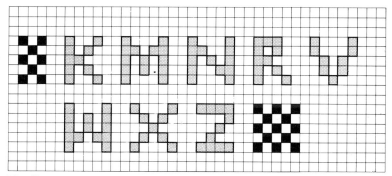

The diagonals

Then there are the remaining letters B, D, G, I, J, Q and Y. B and D need little introductory strokes (as on the typewriter) to distinguish them from 8 or O. G and Q need an extra end line. I and J and Y are individuals:

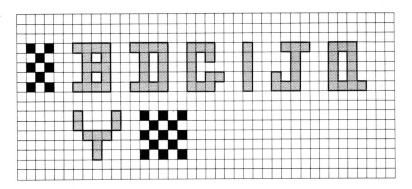

There are many variations of all these letters — here are plain square capitals to start you off. However, you must use a little licence and artistry where needed. D sometimes looks better as and 'I' can be set a throw closer to J than the rules, to avoid too many floating threads. We shall deal with these sorts of problems as they arise.

The first thing to do is to create the empty space in which to put your letters. This means you must get rid of the dark of the chequerboard, exchanging it for light.

Depress the shed with your left hand, and with your right one enter it from the right, hooking up the light threads as you push down their dark partners all the way along. Throw the weft.

Uplift the shed and do the same thing, exchanging the two sets of dark for light in the next row.

Before starting the first letter, you need at least four throws of the plain light background, and this will create floating threads.

FLOATING THREADS

It is unsightly to allow threads to float for more than 3 throws as a general rule, but your letters must appear on a plain ground. I allow two throws between each letter, but between words, and at the start and finish, you must have a longer gap. The start and finish can allow 4 throws without harm. However, you need at least 8 between words, which would be too many.

To get over this difficulty, you must anchor each shed in the gap between the words, and I find the most effective and easiest way is to weave the 2 up-sheds sandwiching the one down-shed of the chequerboard, beating it very tightly. This looks like a flower motif as a punctuation mark, and needs no skill. However, you can make your own design (a thunder flash can look good) provided you include all the threads.

Now you can make the plain background, and you already know how to exchange your colours. To **make your letters** it is simply a matter of writing in your weaving.

To start with A. Look back at your squared letter chart; the first throw must be a solid dark line for the first stroke of the letter. This is the opposite of what you have been doing for the plain background.

Starting with a down-shed, exchange the two groups of light for dark and you will have a solid dark bar.

Coming back on the up-shed, you exchange the first dark group for light, the next light for dark, the second dark for light and the last group of light for dark. You will now have the middle and top bar for the centre of your A.

The down-shed will be a solid dark bar again, and completes the letter.

Sometimes you will find a shed is already made for you. For instance, the down-shed is the middle, or end, throw of an E without any work from you. On the other hand, it may be necessary to change every thread. The amount of work is largely the luck of the draw.

For those of you with literary aspirations, the verses in samplers are popular. You have to précis in order to condense your lines. And your artistic eye will be needed to group the words and fit the whole together. Edge the finished sampler with a simple border to bind it into a framework, and there you may indeed have the makings of an heirloom.

BOLIVIAN PEBBLE WEAVE

SUMMER AND WINTER WITH THE NAVAJO AND HOME FOR CHRISTMAS

This is my very favourite inkle weave. It incorporates so much, and every feature can be individually pursued in its own right, so it is worth while to learn, a pleasure to do, and adaptable for a great many purposes.

To explain my title – it is called a **pebble** weave because the pattern colour appears as a staggered seed or 'pebble' in the background, and is native to the weavers of the Bolivian highlands. **Summer and winter** is the weaver's term for patterns whose colours reverse themselves on the back. What is white on the front patterned in black, in summer and winter also appears black on the back patterned in white.

The Navajos came in because, to show you how, I have started off with a simple Navajo belt pattern based on the triangle and only taking a narrow braid as the easiest demonstration, and **Home for Christmas** is when you have mastered the technique I have shown you, how to adapt it to a very English design of Christmas trees in a lattice work, encouraging you to go on to create other designs for yourselves, not out of Bolivian books but from England or wherever your native home may be.

It is a change from what we have done before; you drop instead of pick up patterns, and you can use extra colours with a visible weft in the work area. But is does require a little more care, since if done too tightly the special weft effect is lost, whilst at the same time your borders must be conventionally crowded for a warp face.

It is advisable to chart your pattern on squared paper before you begin, since each pick of the pattern grows from the previous one and the exact marrying of adjacent warps with the visible spot of weft makes the little 'crow's feet' that are peculiar to the weave. Your 'crows' must

Summer and winter in pebble weave
Charts for both these designs are in the chapter

keep in step. Below I have set out the Navajo design. When you reach the middle, you stand it on its head and work down again. But:

TO WARP Plan your border in the usual way. It is best to keep it plain in order not to detract attention from the patterned area. A plain contrasting stripe on the main background colour is usually best, and throughout the work this is woven warp-faced in the usual inkle manner.

The pattern, which here for this Navajo design is done over 42 pattern threads, alternately contrasts one *double* dark thread with one *single* light. Starting with an open shed (the free threads that are not secured by leashes), warp one double dark thread to one single light leashed thread, ending with the 21st leash on a light thread. Repeat the border on the far side.

METHOD OF WEAVING Using the light yarn for weft, weave the down-shed plain, and within the borders do not crowd too tightly so that

41

you can see the white line of the weft running across.

On the up-shed, drop every other thread – that is to say you drop the first double thread, the 3rd, the 5th, 7th, 9th, and so on across the whole 21.

Come back plain on the down-shed.

On the next up-shed, drop threads 2, 4, 6, 8, etc. – in other words the alternate ones from last time.

Come back plain on the down-shed.

Drop doubles on up-shed alternately
Down-shed plain back except for pattern marked X

Middle

Border

← 21 Pattern ends on each shed →

42

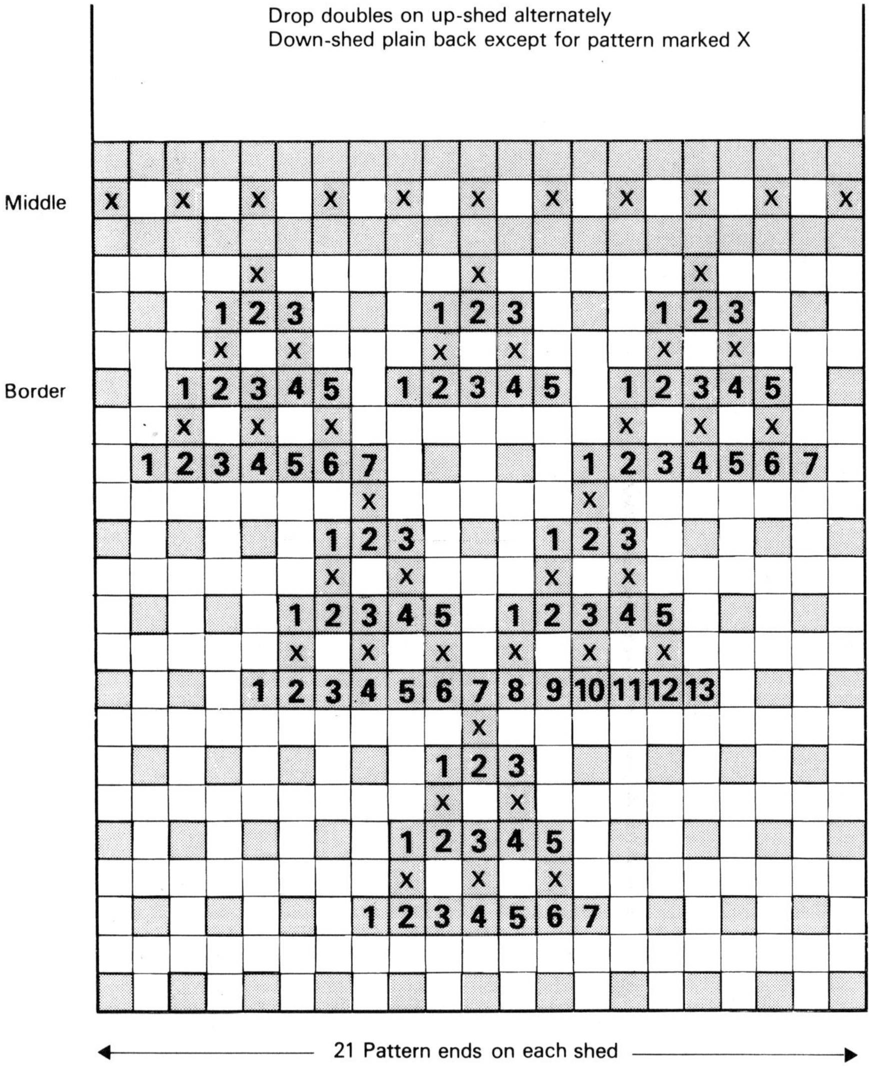

These four rows are the background that you will continue doing throughout, and you will see at once the little white 'crow's feet' criss-cross effect, with the spot or 'pebble' of the dark colour.

To impose your design on this background, you pick up on the down-shed those otherwise dropped threads as you need them, and on the up-shed you drop the dark threads lying in between them, so that the warps are split apart – in fact, as you do a sort of basket weave on the background, so you do another more concentrated basket weave on the actual pattern.

I have charted the pattern for you. Where you have a block of threads picked up adjacent, I have written in the number, so that starting at the right hand side you know at once you must pick up the next 5 or 7 or whatever threads without having to count the squares.

The crosses on the down-shed are the threads you pick up.

When you have completed the pattern and turn it over, you will see the exact replica, 'crow's feet' and all, reversed in colour on the back – what was dark is now light, and vice versa.

HOME FOR CHRISTMAS

Here is another chart for Christmas trees (p. 44). At first you may find it confusing that the lattice uses the pebbles here and there to make itself, but this is simplified by the numbers to count in the margin before you make the design.

Incidentally, the back of this pattern is particularly pretty, and is often regarded as the front face.

This particular pattern was joined matching the empty triangles to make a tabard. You could, however, ring the changes by putting summer against winter, or head to tail!.

As long as you warp the requisite number of pattern ends for your design, you can easily portray not only llamas, as the Bolivians do, but very English animals such as dogs or rabbits. Cross-stitch designs can be easily adapted as long as you remember there is a line between each cross-stitch pattern line to accommodate the second shed.

The background alone is pretty enough to pursue, and changing the weft, either on the background alone to get coloured checks, or at the end of each pattern section to get a differently coloured pattern, can be effective. It gives you an additional colour dimension. Perhaps you can see why it is my favourite weave.

Clear acr

9

14
13
11
10
13
6

RAGS

Rag weaving is not usually associated with inkle weaving, but it can be done with great success. The American weaver, Mary Meigs Atwater, when asked to weave rags, said: 'If this distressful thing MUST be done . . .'! I do agree that merely to make one rag out of several others is vice and not virtue, – and all too often found – but it can be done very attractively, and has the advantage of using up remnants at no cost. There is such a variety in rags, and how you can use them, that it is a study in itself.

The early North Americans, the Scandinavians, the Greek peasants in particular were and are adept at weaving bright and beautiful articles from discarded cottons, and with expertise all manner of weaving techniques can be practised and lovely results achieved.

The problem with the inkle loom is that it gives a warp-faced weave, and in rag weaving it is the weft that must give patterning. The trick is to convert the weave.

Using strong rug-warping cotton or linen, you must space out your warp threads widely, as in a rug or tapestry weave, if you are to reveal its thicker weft. However, even with the notched upper peg that the best inkle looms now have, this is very hard to do. Since the strain is on the pull of the warp across the pegs, however carefully you space your threads they crowd in on themselves immediately you begin to weave, and you find you are back with a warp-face.

But there is a way, and it is very simple.

SPACED WARPS

Find a piece of ¾ in. (18mm) tubing. If the centre of used wool cheeses are large enough – they must be ¾ in. (18mm) inside diameter to fit the

Mary Meigs Atwater
The 'Mother' of US inkle weaving, authoress of *Shuttlecraft* and *Byways in Handweaving* (who could not abide rag weaving), at an old Gilmore inkle loom.
　　Note that she has converted the loom to take rollers for greater lengths of warp, so it is not strictly inkle (with continuous warp)!
　　In 1946, she and Harriet Tidball visited Guatemala, whence her interest in back-strap and inkle weaving came, and I felt any book on inkle weaving should pay her some homage, hence this historic photograph.

usual inkle peg – they are ideal. Alternatively, a small piece of plastic or rubber ¾ in. (18mm) tubing, such as garden hose, will do.

The trick is to cut your hosing/tubing into ½ in. (12mm) rings. I used 18 rings in all.

As you start to warp, you now slip one of these rings onto the notched peg after each leash thread, and similarly one over the leash peg after securing each leash as you go. This will space the warp widely, firmly and uniformly.

The ideal material to start with is the better parts of old printed cotton clothing; the smaller the pattern in the print, the nicer it will look. You must cut, or tear, the cotton into long strips about 1 in. (25mm) wide. Unless you are striving for a ragged, rather unfinished look, take care to fold the rough edges in. This can be done with an iron before weaving, or arranged in the shed as you go along.

You will quickly get the feel of different materials and how best to deal

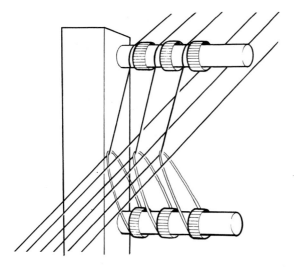

Showing how the rings put on after each leash thread and each leash separate the warp for a rag weave.

with them. The folding is unnecessary with woollens that have been closely woven in the first instance, if they are cut and not ripped.

Bearing in mind that a pattern of stripes, if such you want, will be contained in the braid, so you are about to weave more vertically than horizontally as on a conventional loom, you want to be bold about the areas of material you use. Once you have adjusted yourself to this 'other way round' approach in design, you will find patterning in checks very easy. Squares on the braid, when joined with other squared braids make very effective patchwork designs, and use up small amounts of material skilfully.

Besides colour patterns, textures can be interesting. I did a bathmat with old terry-towelling and linen sheeting, using them in alternate sheds with two shuttles and firmly beating down. The result was a honeycomb weave, the terry standing up high and the linen, which was folded smooth, lying smooth.

Printed fabrics make their own patterns for you in the plain weave, and by varying the thickness of the strip used, you can thicken and enlarge your work, or fine it down.

As North American rag-weaving is different to Scandinavian, and Greek rag-weaving different to both in the ways the fabrics are handled, so too can inkle-ragging develop a character of its own far from the 'distressing thing' Mary Meigs Atwater feared.

Instant patchwork
Cushion woven from scraps on a red/white warp, finished
with red piping

FROM RAGS TO PATCHES

Inevitably, one thing leads to another, and having spaced warps to take rags, you can have a great deal of enjoyment spacing warps in the same way to take yarns.

One of the most useful and colourful ways to use spaced warps is to make patchwork out of yarn ends – those odd pieces not long enough to do much else with. If you warp with a fine linen thread, and use thicker coloured wefts, the warp is practically invisible. You will have patches of bright colours, which, when your strip is cut into pieces and joined, give instant patchwork of a different texture and nature than the rag ones.

If you use warp of alternate colours – for example, red and white threads – of the same thickness of the weft, all the weft colours are tinged, at a distant viewing, with the red shade and dappled with the white.

On the next go, try to use the same weft colours on a green and white, or blue and white, warp, and you will see how the same weft colours all undergo a subtle change.

This is a useful exercise, as it uses up scraps from knitting and crochet too short for any part of a warp, and far from being simply a clean-up of the workbag, it can be very attractive.

CHRISTMAS TIME

CARDS BY THE YARD

Your inkle loom should come into its own at Christmas. Gifts that can be quickly and attractively made are endless — all manner of bags and cushions in wool — spectacle cases and bookmarks in fine silks — belts and dog collars and leads in string or cotton — each one individual and unique.

Why not weave your *Christmas cards* by the yard? It is original, thrifty, fun and usually appreciated!

This is the recipe for a little Christmas tree in a red pot that goes very fast and easily. I used red, white and black mercerised cotton, but it would look lovely in silks.

TO WARP   23 leashes

W		W		R		W		W		Repeat	W		until		W		W		R		W		W
	W		W		R		W		B				B	15 in all		W		R		W		W

Using a white weft, weave 8 weft throws. This gives you black and white stripes within a border of a red line on a white ground.

You start your tree upside down.

On the next down-shed, pick up the central black thread.

Come back plain on the up-shed.

On the 2nd down-shed, pick up the 2 black threads either side of the central one you picked up last time.

Come back plain on the up-shed.

On the 3rd down-shed, pick up the central thread again and the two either side of it.

Come back plain on the up-shed.

On the 4th down-shed, pick up the same 2 threads astride the central thread and the two outside them.

50

Come back plain.

Continue like this, enlarging the pick-up area until you have done 7 pick-up rows. This is the tree top.

On the next down-shed row, insert with a threaded needle a red thread, entering from behind between the red threads in your border and bringing the needle out in front after the centre black thread, which is picked up.

Weave 3 more throws, still picking up this central thread, so that it floats for 4 rows of weave.

Using the needle, wrap the red yarn round and round this central floating thread. This is the trunk of your tree.

On the next weft throw, run the red needle through with the weft to within 4 threads of the black and white area margin. The white weft goes the whole length as before.

You now do a shortened form of 'Sumac' with the red yarn. A true Sumac stitch goes over 4 and under 2 all along the line. Here you take the red thread and go over 2 and under one – a sort of overstitch – to the last 4 threads of the black and white.

Change sheds, throw the white weft right across, and take the red needle over 2 and under one across as before.

Repeat this line twice more. This is the red pot.

At the end of the last Sumac, run the needle through the rest of the shed to the red line on the border, where you take it out invisibly to the back. The start and end of the red thread is shaved off eventually and becomes invisible in the red line.

Weave 8 rows plain. Finish off by taking the last weft under the last throw. Insert a tiny piece of cardboard and begin the next card.

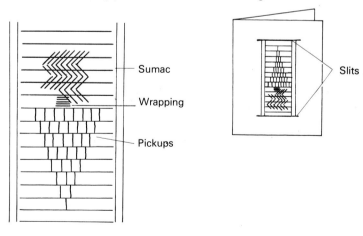

Sumac

Wrapping

Pickups

Slits

You cut the whole into sections where you pull out the cardboard pieces. Allowing for wastage in the working area, you should get approximately 20 cards on a full warp.

Cut two slits in a blue, green or red card, and slip the Christmas tree through.

HANGING CHRISTMAS TREES

And here is another sort of Christmas tree.

It can be hung from a light above the dining-room table as a centrepiece for Christmas parties. A friend who keeps a shop strung a row of them across her shop window on a string. You will have your own ideas what to do with them.

Showing a class I began by cutting up a bamboo place-mat. A student went home and managed with a lot less complication, simply cutting a stick from her hedge and slicing it into ever increasing lengths. This answered admirably and made a much larger tree than my bamboo slivers. You may wish to follow her example, but I will show you how I did mine, in case you haven't a hedge and do have a bamboo place-mat.

One mat will give you four trees.

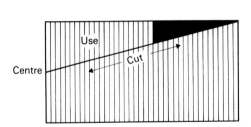

Mark the centre of the short end of the mat, and cut it across to the far end. Discard the very short pieces at the far edge as shown.

TO WARP   18 leashes. Alternate red and gold threads.

Shiny rayon or bright mercerised cotton is best in two festive colours. I used red and gold, but red and green, or silver tinsel and red would be nice and bright. The finished braid is going to twist, and so two colours show first one, then the other, in a spiral, and you want them gay and glittery. The braid should be about 1 in. (25mm) wide.

(If you are using the sticks from your hedge in a larger version of course you will need greater width.)

Weave for about 2 in. (50mm). You will have red and gold stripes.

Instead of the next weft throw, insert the shortest bamboo stick.

Change the shed and throw the weft normally, pulling it tight around the stick and beating it in heftily.

Insert the next shortest stick instead of the next weft.

Change shed and throw the weft as before.

You continue like this, substituting a stick for every alternate weft, until they are all used up. As the sticks get longer, they will stick out further away from the base of the loom like this:

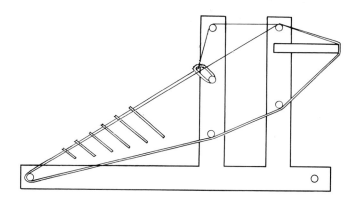

One side of the work will have red threads across the sticks, and the other side will have gold, and the sticks will be very close together.

(You may want to space them further apart: certainly, if they are the thicker sticks from your hedge! but if you are to get the spiral colour change you must stick to this colour set-up, so add **uneven** throws of weft between the sticks, never even ones or the sticks will be red and gold on the same side.)

Weave a few more plain throws to lock the last stick in firmly, and finish off, leaving a 3 in. (75mm) fringe.

When you cut the braid off the loom, push alternate sticks through to the left instead of the right, so you form an equilateral triangle so:

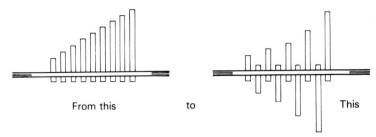

From this   to   This

Tie or braid the fringe at the top into a loop for hanging, and fix a Christmas bauble, bell or tassel in the fringe at the bottom. Hang it up by the loop and twist. The red and gold twisting inside the sticks looks gay, and you further decorate by hanging tiny glass balls or tinsel on the ends of the sticks. If you use cocktail sticks instead of a bamboo mat, you can spear coloured sweeties on the stick ends. If you opted for the larger hedgerow stick, you could use Christmas tree ornaments. It's an idea you will find plenty of scope in experimenting with — novel and thrifty and attractive.

DYEING FOR A DIAGONAL

This is a little digression on a diagonal track. It involves dyeing, or at least inking, your warp, so if you are not that sort of a person, skip this chapter.

I came upon this technique by chance. After seeing some ikats from central Asia, I realised my inkle discovery could emulate and digress upon the Asian technique, which called for warp-faced narrow bands, the pattern dyed in the warp, joined head to toe, or side to side. An inkle loom can supply these conditions, and adds a distinctive flavour which is solely its own.

EXPLOITING UNEVEN SHEDS

The secret lies in the inkle loom having **uneven sheds**. The leash threads, by reason of their going over the upper peg and being pulled down again, are just that little bit longer than the open threads. It is this feature peculiar to the inkle loom that makes this diagonal technique possible.

TO BEGIN   To make your warp for dyeing, you have various options, but we will start with the two simplest possibilities. You can wind the

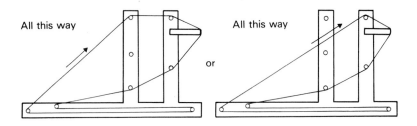

All this way   or   All this way

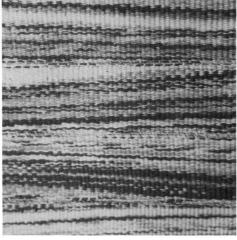

Diagonals
The braid has been cut into four pieces, which
were then joined head to tail for the zig-zag
effect. Woven in cotton

entire warp as for the top shed only. Alternatively wind it all on the lower
shed only. That is: either wind all potential leash threads, or all potential
open threads.

To ensure that the threads will not tangle or cross when they are off the
loom, stick one or two pieces of Sellotape across the warp while it is still
taut on the loom.

Release the tension adjuster, so you can slip the warp easily off the

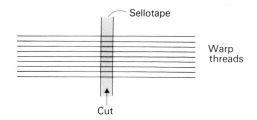

loom, and stretch it tight across a board or table for dyeing. It will lie as a loop which can be dyed as it is, or you can slip a piece of plastic down the centre and dye each side individually. This time leave it as it is.

Let us suppose the dyeing is simply to print 3 broad horizontal stripes next to each other across the warp at any point – three different colours about 3 in. (75mm) wide will illustrate what happens clearly.

When the paint, ink, or dye has dried, pull off the Sellotape and wind the warp into a ball, so that you may once again put it back onto the loom, only this time with the two sheds in the proper manner for weaving. What happens is due to that tiny difference in the length of the two sheds. Your horizontal lines creep forward by that fraction on each thread. When rewound onto the loom, the three horizontal lines will become a long diagonal stripe that runs from one edge of the warp across to the other, effecting the maximum elongation. The pattern walks up your warp for you, and with no hard line but a jagged step staggered by the tiny differential of the creep.

Similarly, different horizontal bars on different parts of the warp will make other diagonal lines that will cross each other, which if done in varying colours can be very effective.

This is at its simplest – the dyeing on the one warp threading. With an inkle loom, it is no hardship to re-wind this same warp after the first dyeing on the other shed for newly angled diagonals to offset the original ones. Each shed may also be wound first clockwise, and then anti-clockwise to get diagonals running from right to left as well as left to right. With practice, and a little geometry, you can progress from mere horizontal bars to shapes and angles that not only cross and re-cross each other but contrast in the degree of their slope, and colour can be made to run into colour on a single thread in a way you cannot achieve by an overall dye, so that the pattern will paint itself – blue thread running into red making purple, yellow into blue for green etc. and nowhere in the warp does the pattern stay still but creeps on.

APPLYING THE DYE   I do not like dipping warp into a dye bath, because it is so definite. If dye is pressed into the warp threads with a sponge through a stencil cut from thin cardboard (cereal packets are perfect) the result can be made patchy or complete to order, and if a patchy effect is achieved, the result is unique. The resultant colour is mottled, which will soften the diagonals and allows the creeping colours to blend more subtly.

When making up, an occasional conventionally straight-patterned, or plain, woven strip set among the diagonal ones, which are sewn together head to toe, both frame them and make for interest in the overall pattern. (This can also be achieved by setting groups of plain undyed threads in groups among the dyed ones when you warp for weaving.)

On the other hand, a rather splendid length of cloth made entirely of the dyed strips has the overall effect of a watermark on fine Indian paper, or watered silk, and the variation is limitless.

And while the mathematicians are fascinated by computing their angles and directions, the people who like to colour haphazardly and hope for the best produce just as successful a result.

It was all exciting to me because I discovered a unique use for the inkle loom all due to that tiny difference in the length of its two sheds.

WEFTS

We have said very little about wefts, because they are for the most part invisible in inkle weaving. Nevertheless, they play their part. We have already found that a thick weft is more suitable for a carpet, a thin one better for pick-ups, and the weft plays an important role in the Bolivian pebble weave. However, there is more to them than that.

SUPPLEMENTARY WEFTS

A supplementary weft can be all the decoration needed for a lampshade trimming. Run a group of silk threads (or a thick cotton one) in with a normal shed of weaving. Weave plain for 4 rows, and then send the supplementary weft across again, leaving it on the side for another 4 rows, and back it can go once more. This technique can be used to make a ridge pattern with a scallop effect staggered up the side of your braid, and done in shiny silks or rayons with a matt cotton makes an effective trimming.

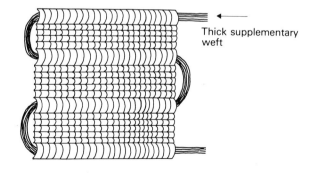

Thick supplementary weft

Thick and thin wefts
A plainweave strip patterned by thick and thin
wefts, woven by Kay Kettle

INSERTIONS

This same idea can be exploited without the scalloped sides by inserting small pieces of thick material in the sheds at varying intervals as you weave. Each piece is safely locked in by the next shed change, and it can be done either at random, or in an arranged patterned plan.

Where rigidity as well as decoration is needed, you can insert sticks, or a flat slither of wood, threading it in and out the threads of the shed to

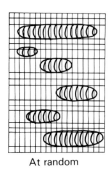
At random

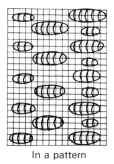
In a pattern

show as much of it as you desire. It is locked securely in by the next shed change.

Showing different parts of the sticks in their different sheds can make intriguing patterns, and the braids can be joined together to make original place-mats.

FLOATING WEFTS

However, there is yet another way that wefts come into their own – as floating wefts. If you look closely at much early Chinese silken weaving, you will see that an almost embroidered look is often achieved by using weft threads. It is usually done so finely and with such skill that the only way to see it is not embroidered is to turn it over and find no mark of the

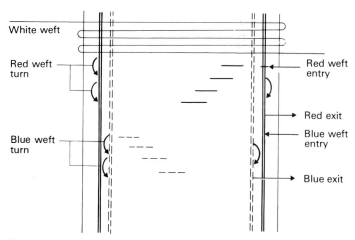

Showing floating wefts
This diagram shows the paths of the white, red and blue wefts individually, though they perform simultaneously.

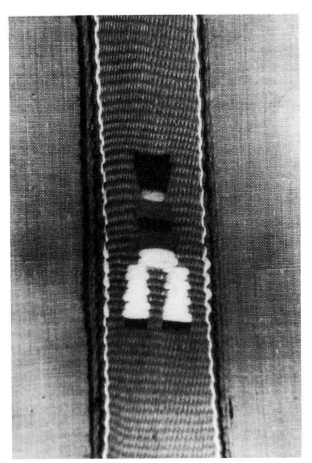

Floating wefts
Blue warp with red, white and
black weft floats turned in their
own margins

design on the back at all, showing a needle never pierced the cloth. Let
us try the same thing on the inkle loom.

As you know, the only place a weft shows in a plain inkle weave is
where it turns the corner at the side of the work to enter the next shed. If
we use two colours of weft – red and blue – on a white ground, this will
mean a red and a blue as well as a white shuttle of yarn, and they all
three will have to turn the corner. To avoid having all three colours
showing at the edge of the braid, you have to provide turning points for
the red and the blue inside the work.

This is done by warping a completely white braid with a red line and a blue line (2 threads each) running down the inside edges. These two lines on each side will be the turning points for the red weft and the blue weft respectively, leaving the white one to turn invisibly at the outside edges in the normal way. You are, after all, weaving a white braid, with the red and blue simply decorating it.

For your first pattern, let us suppose you want a red line to cross a blue line as an X on the white ground.

After you have thrown your white weft across, also enter the red weft into the shed NOT at the edge of the braid but at the red line. Take it under the first 3 threads of the shed, and then take it out towards you over the next 4 threads before re-entering the shed again and running through it to the red line at the other side, when you will lift it out again.

Still in the same shed, enter the blue yarn at the blue line on the opposite side, and run it across the whole shed to the last 7 threads before the lines, where you lift it out for 4 threads and back for the last 3 before lifting it out on the far side of the blue lines. (This will be the side the other two threads entered from.)

Change the shed and throw the white weft right across.

Turning the red yarn on the red border thread, run it across the shed until it is 8 threads from the coloured border lines, lift it out for 4 threads, and enter it back for 4 before you lift it out around its red border thread.

Still in this shed, enter the blue yarn around its border thread, under 4 threads, lift it out for 4, and then into the shed and across to its blue border thread.

With the white weft running right across each time in the normal way, continue with the two colours, moving them a thread along each row and turning them in their own colour lines, until they have crossed each other and gone to the opposite side from where they started.

These coloured weft threads need to be thick enough – and doubled thin thread is preferable to single heavy thread – to hide the warp threads under them completely.

If you turn the braid over and look underneath, you will find no trace of red or blue – it is completely white, like the old Chinese seemingly embroidered, but actually woven, silks.

In the spaces where you don't want coloured patterning, you can lift the colours – or one colour only perhaps – out at its colour line. When the work is completed, you simply shave off the tails of coloured thread on the lines where they originally went in, and finally came out, and they will not show, and only someone who knows how to do this will be able to tell where you turned the corners to take the next shed in the weaving with your coloured threads.

BEADWORK

You can use your inkle loom to weave with beads, which is a craft on its own. Here your weft turns into a threaded needle on which you also thread the beads, laying each bead **between** the spaced warp threads as you lay the needle in the shed. Pull the needle and thread through the beads so positioned, and change the shed to do the same again with more beads on the needle. Each change of shed locks in the beads of the one before held on their thread between the warps.

It is not inkle weaving, but I mention it since for those who wish to try, it can be done upon your inkle loom.

ALL MANNER OF THINGS

One of the rewards of teaching weaving is the variety of ideas you gather from your students. Many of mine have been skilled needlewomen, and thus able to bring their other skills to the making-up and finishing of their work. I thought it might be helpful to tell you of some of the successful, and sometimes surprising, results.

MOCCASIN SLIPPERS

I had told this particular class about an exhibition then on of Uzbekistan work, in which were shown exquisitely woven boots. To the next lesson came this pair of slippers.

TO START THE SLIPPER   First the sole – This was simply made as in a French espadrille. Plait a thick braid, and, laying it flat on a table, curl it so

and stitch it firmly along the coils.
(An alternative to this would be to weave a tube on your loom, running a thick cord up the centre to give it added strength and bulk, and coil the tube instead of the plait.)

THE MOCCASIN UPPERS   Weave two short braids about 2–2½ in. (50–62mm) wide, each long enough to divide into a main piece to run around the sole and also a small end about 4 in. (100mm) long with the end fringe.

Wind the main piece around the sole, starting and ending at the centre of the heel back. This can be left as a fringe, or sewn under, to please yourself.

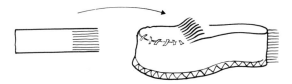

Insert the small end of the braid, moccasin fashion into the toe, and flap the fringe over its end.

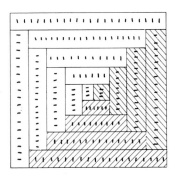

This pair of moccasin slippers was woven from oddments left over from a rug, in 2 ply rug wool.

A LOG CABIN PATCHWORK CUSHION

Another pupil, who was gifted at patchwork, used two quite narrow braids in different shades of blue — one braid in light shades and the other dark — to make a cushion in the log cabin patchwork design.

STUFFED BANDS

Another clever idea was a padded liner for a garden chair. Pairs of short bands were sewn together and stuffed, and joined to each other until the resulting mattress was long enough. It made a very comfortable garden seat, which was easily rolled up and brought inside at the end of the day.

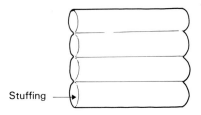

Stuffing

WOVEN BANDS

The bands themselves can be interwoven for a strong seat for a stool or collapsible garden chair.

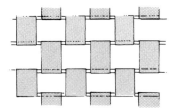

AN EVENING BAG

There are, of course, a myriad of ways to make up braids for bags of all sorts, but this is a particularly quick and pretty little evening bag, which looks expensive but is not at all.

You will need a card of 2 in. (50mm) wide velvet ribbon (which can be had very inexpensively from Woolworths in various colours). Black was my choice. Also a card of gold (or silver or bronze) wrapping string from a newsagent for tying up Christmas parcels. This is very much cheaper than costly goldfingering yarns, and does the job just as well. Finally a ball of black twisted rayon.

Weave 45 in. (1143mm) of braid in the black twisted rayon, using the gold wrapping string for your pattern – a chain with a little chequerboard and another chain motif is pretty. When finished, cut it into three, and join the pieces with a band of the velvet ribbon between each woven band. Line it, if you like, and fold it into a pochette, sewing up the sides. The flap can be finished with an edging of crochet in the gold, and it really is very effective.

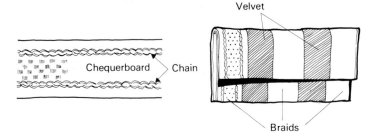

ANOTHER QUICK EVENING BAG

This is another pretty little evening bag with the minimum of make-up.
For evening purposes, use coloured cotton or rayon or silky yarns. Warp
as wide a band as is comfortable to weave (5 in. (125mm) is the usual
limit) and cut it into two uneven lengths, about 32 in. (800mm) and 28
in. (700mm). Sew these pieces into two uneven loops, and join them
halfway up the longest loop. Slip the long loop through the short one,
and hang it on your wrist.

This can also be made in heavier wools for day use, and it is surprising
how much can be carried in it. Because of the speed in making up, it is a
favourite for bazaars.

PURSE/PENCIL CASE

Cut a brightly coloured braid into 12 in. (300mm) lengths. Fold them
double, seam the open end and put a zip along the top.

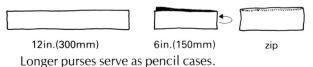

12in.(300mm)   6in.(150mm)   zip

Longer purses serve as pencil cases.

SHOULDER AND SHOPPING BAGS

The variety of these seems limitless. They may have gussets, or no gussets; long tube handles, or short tube handles; and gussets that become flat woven handles and then gussets again down the far side.

The braids may go vertically or horizontally.

There is a saddle bag shape that can be large enough to hang over your bicycle carrier, or small enough (in silk) for evening use.

You can decorate in colour, or texture, or both.

You can join the braids invisibly, by linking the weft loops at the braid edges to each other.

Or you can make a feature of them by joining them in a flat seam down the edge of two braid thicknesses, and open them with the ridges outwards. These ribs give a bit of body to the shape and add interest to the overall pattern.

You will have your own ideas.

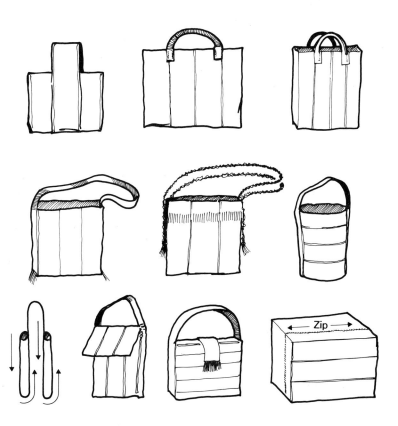

FURNISHINGS

Cushions can be woven in all shapes and designs, and finished with narrow tubing, which can also be used to edge stools, chairs, etc.

Curtain ties are prettiest when made of fine silk or rayon with thicker wefts to emphasise the shed changes.

I had one pupil cover all her dining-room chairs in a marled wool, doing a pick-up of every fourth thread, staggering it every other row like a basketwork, which was quite beautiful.

Another pupil covered a screen frame with unjoined strips, as a room divider.

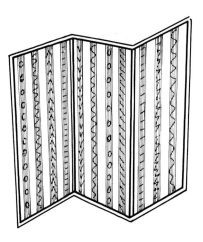

And, of course, *wall hangings* come in all colours and techniques, and can look very striking in fine strong-coloured cottons. My favourite, however, was in plain linen with wrapped warps at random – in reality wrapped to a careful design but giving an impression of careless art.

CLOTHING

Clothing can be made. In the main, an inkle loom is better geared to decorating rather than making the whole fabric of clothes, but I have seen lovely tabards and ponchos, waistcoats and jackets, and a splendid coat with the arms running right across the yoke in one piece. One must admit that this sort of enterprise is easier done on a large loom, but there are plenty of decorative ideas suited to your inkle loom.

A most successful one was a waistband in two reds that topped a black evening skirt, and from which hung more red bands at 3 in. (75mm) intervals all around which fell to the skirt hem. They were only attached to the waistband, so they flared out and moved when the wearer walked, and complemented with a pochette handbag in the same reds, the effect was stunning.

Another development of this same swinging bands effect was achieved by a long waistcoat, whose bands were only joined to the waist and hung free below, like a grass skirt, showing glimpses of the skirt underneath when the wearer moved.

It gives a handknitted cardigan or jacket a professional and distinctive look to edge it with a narrow woven strip of its own wool. Buttonholes can be made vertically by introducing a second weft (as shown in the chapter on Mechanics). Save small pieces to run across pocket tops and cuff the sleeves.

VALEDICTION

The preceding chapters of this book comprise the course of instruction I try to give to serious inkle weavers. As in every craft, it is you, yourself – your ideas and your willingness to experiment in expressing your own creativity – that make for success. The teacher can but show you how to use the tool. It is up to you to put that use to good effect.

You should by now have a more than ordinary working skill with an inkle loom, and I do hope you will fruitfully enjoy using it.

The keynote of my instruction has been in **free-fingering**. I have met inkle weavers laboriously, needlessly, inserting rigid heddles, or count- less additional groups of leashes, to achieve the effects we have painlessly covered in these pages simply by using our fingers. If you bear in mind that every thread is within your reach, and be ready to do with it as you will, you will have mastered the craft of inkle weaving.

HOW TO MAKE YOUR OWN INKLE LOOM

After many years of experimenting with inkle loom design, and consulting with a vast variety of weavers, my husband finally produced the Bradley inkle loom. It is strong, compact, light, mobile, dismountable and good-looking, and for these reasons you can find it in homes, schools, colleges, hospitals, workshops and it is even found on board ships out in the North Sea!

Its measurements allow **the leashes** to be warped, cut and tied on the loom itself.

The **tension adjuster**, being a non-slip cam type, is accurate and easy to use, and positioned near the working area. It gives a generous play of 3 in. (75mm).

You have a long section of the work **visible** as it progresses.

And you can choose from a variety of **warp lengths** up to a maximum of 9 ft. (2.77m).

If you are to do a good job, you must have a good tool. There are kits, and instructions, of how to make inkle looms, and I have met the results of some of these in my classes and almost always found them, at very best, restricting. We feel that the Bradley design below is the best possible.

MATERIALS

LUMBER
One piece 28 in. (710mm) x 1⅝ in. (40mm) x 1⅝ in. (40mm) for the base
Two pieces 14 in. (355mm) x 1⅝ in. (40mm) x 1⅝ in. (40mm) for the 2 uprights

Two pieces 10 in. (250mm) x 1¼ in. (31mm) x ⅜ in. (9mm) for the 2 feet
One block 4 in. (100mm) x 5⅞ in. (150mm) x ¾ in. (18mm) for the tension adjuster
6 ft. (1.85m) of ¾ in. (18mm) dowelling for the pegs

HARDWARE
One round head bolt 8 in. (200mm) x ⅜ in. (9mm)
Two round head machine screws ¼ in. (6mm) x 2 in. (50mm)
One ⅜ in. (9mm) wing nut
Two ¼ in. (6mm) wing nuts
Four ¼ in. (6mm) steel washers
One ⅜ in. (9mm) steel washer
Two ¼ in. (6mm) spring washers
One leather (or rubber) washer 1½ in. (38mm) x ⅜ in. (9mm)
Four ¾ in. (18mm) x No. 8 screws

Use Douglas Fir or Canadian Pine. A hardwood is too heavy.

METHOD

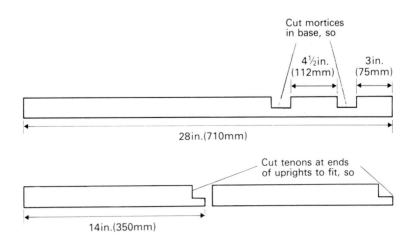

Following the diagrams, bore holes for pegs, 1 in. (25mm) deep and ¾ in. (18mm) diameter.

● *Base*: shown viewed from the right side, and viewed from top. Bore 3 holes.

● *Front upright*: shown front and sideview – 3 holes.

● *Back upright*: shown front and sideview – 2 holes.

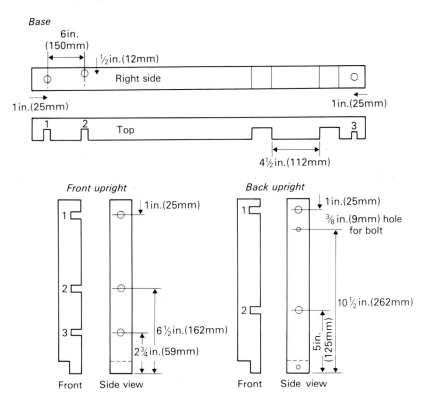

Lay the two uprights, holes down, side by side, the back one in front of the front one, as shown.

Bore a ¾ in. (9mm) hole 2½ in. (62mm) deep, which will completely hole the back upright, and enter the front upright by ⅞ in. (22mm). They must be perfectly aligned since a connecting dowel will enter these holes.

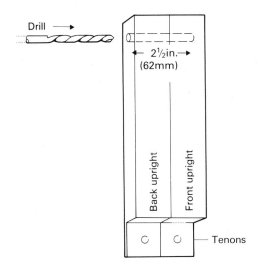

THE PEGS

Cut the dowelling into nine 7 in. (175mm) lengths.
Insert one piece between the uprights.
Into each hole in base and uprights, thoroughly glue and tap each dowel
home. Check with tri-square they are at right angles to frame.

TENSION BLOCK

Bore a ⅜ in. (9mm) hole for the tension adjuster bolt in the back upright,
10½ in. (262mm) from its base.

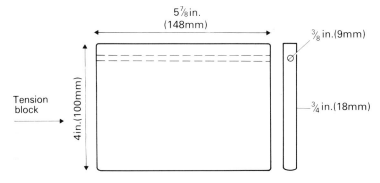

Round the edge of the tension block, and bore ⅜ in. (9mm) hole ¾ in.
(18mm) from top.

ASSEMBLY

Hold base in bench vice with holes uppermost. Tap the two uprights endwise into the mortices until firmly seated. Bore ¼ in. (6mm) holes through each mortice. With washer on machine screw, tap through from peg side, add further washer and spring washer on other end and tighten with wing nut for each upright.

Push bolt through back upright, put on leather (or rubber) washer, tension block, ¾ in. (18mm) steel washer and ¾ in. (18mm) wing nut.

Screw the two feet under the base 5 in. (125mm) in from either end, with two No. 8 screws for each foot.

2 pieces 10in.(254mm)×1¼in.(31mm)
×⅜in.(9mm) for feet

FOOTNOTE

This loom is obtainable from:
Bradley Inkle Looms,
82 North Lane,
East Preston,
Sussex BN16 1HE

GLOSSARY

Beat Push down the weft into the warp against the woven area — usually done with the edge of the shuttle, or small stick or hand

Crowded Warp Where the weft is pulled so tight that the warp threads are tightly packed, ie: crowded one on top of another.

Ikat Derived from **Mengikat** (Malayan and Indonesian), meaning to tie or bind, and refers to strips of fabric where the warp (in Turkestan and Asia generally) or the weft (in Bali) or both warp and weft are tie-dyed before weaving. Origins ancient and uncertain, but believed to be Indian, whence it spread throughout Asia.

Inkle A linen band or drawstring (*Webster's Dictionary*) From early spellings such as ynchull, ynkell, ynkle, ynckle, inckle and incle. Dutch is possible origin (*Oxford English Dictionary*). Early examples of use: 1541: 'for a pece or brode yncull for gyrdlls' . . .
1567: 'With baskets . . . on their arms, wherein they haue laces, pynnes, nedles, white ynkell' . . .
Shakespeare in *The Winter's Tale* has a servant say of Autolycus: 'Hath ribbons of all colours i the rainbow, points . . . inkles, caddysses, camricks, lawnes.'

Leash Loop which pulls down alternate threads on loom so the weaving sheds may be made. Synonymous with heddle on other looms.

Shed The space in the warp between threads through which the weft passes, made by lowering or uplifting the unleashed, or open threads.

Shuttle Instrument for holding weft so it can be passed easily through the warp.

Tension Stress put on the warp by stretching it along the loom.

Warp Lengthwise threads along the loom into which the weft is woven.

Warp-faced A weave showing only the warp threads.

Weft The threads woven horizontally in and out the warp to make the fabric.

Weft-faced A weave showing only the weft threads (like tapestry).

SELECT BIBLIOGRAPHY

Atwater, Mary Meigs, *Byways in Handweaving*, Macmillan, New York, 1954.

Casson, Marjorie and Cahlander, Adele, *The Art of Bolivian Highland Weaving*, Watson-Guptill, New York 1976.

Pendleton, Mary, *Navajo & Hopi Weaving Techniques*, Studio Vista, London, 1974.

Tacker, Harold and Sylvia, *Band Weaving*, Studio Vista, London, 1974.

Tidball, Harriet, *Weaving Inkle Bands*, Shuttle Craft Guild, Monograph 37, Lansing, Michigan, 1969.

Trotzig, Liv and Axelsson, Astrid, *Weaving Bands*, Van Nostrand Reinhold, New York, 1974.

INDEX

A

Afro style, belt, necklace, 31, 33, 34
Atwater, Mary Meigs, 45–7

B

Backstop, 11
Bags, evening, quick evening, saddle, shopping, shoulder, 67–9
Bazaar Purse, 68
Beads, 64
Belt: Afro, 34; Lettered, 35
Bolivian Pebble Weave, 40–4
Bookmarkers, lettered, 35
Buttonholes, 19, 71

C

Charts: Christmas trees in lattice (pebble weave), 43; Peruvian design (intensive
  pick-up), 27; Summer/winter Navajo (pebble weave), 42
Chequerboard: for evening bag, 67–8; for lettering, 35–6
Christmas cards, by the yard, 50–1
Christmas trees: hanging, 52–4; in latticework, 43–4
Clothing, 70–1
Coat, 14, 70
Curtain ties, 70
Curves, 17
Cushions, 48, 70
Cutting braids, 20
Cutting threads for shaping, 16

D

Diagonals, to exploit uneven sheds, 55–6
Dyeing, applying dye, 58

E

Edging: cardigans, 19, 71; lampshades, 18, 19
Evening bags, 67–8

F

Floating threads, 38

Index   Floating wefts, 30, 61
Fraying ends, to prevent, 20
Fringes, 18
Furnishings, 70

G
Gilmore, E. E., 2
Gussets, 69

H
Handles, 17
How to make your own inkle loom, 73—7

I
Ikats, 55
Insertions, weft, 60—1
Instant fringes, 18
Instant patchwork, 47—8

J
Jackets, 70

K
Knubbling knots, 29—30

L
Leashes, how to make, 5—6
Lettering, 35—9
Log cabin patchwork cushion, 66
Loops, as edging, 18—19

M
Moccasin slippers, 65—6

N
Navajo design, 40—1
Necklace: Afro, 32—4; wrapped warp, 32—4

O
Odds and ends, use of, 28, 29, 49
Old English inkle loom, 2

P
Patchwork, instant for cushion, 47—8
Pebble weave, 40—4
Pencil case, 68
Peruvian design, 26—7
Pick-ups: double, 23; intensive, 23—7; simple, 21—2
Plainweave, 15
Ponchos, 70
Pulling warp around loom, 12
Purse, 68

Q
Quick evening bag, 68

R
Rag weaving, 45–7
Rubbish rug, 28

S
Samplers, 35, 39
Scallops, 18
Scottish braid loom, 1
Screen, 70
Sculptured braids, 18
Securing ends, 13
Shaping, 16
Shopping bags, 69
Shoulder bags, 69
Slits, 19
Stuffed bands, 66–7
Summer/winter weave, 40–4
Supplementary wefts, 59

T
Tabards, 45, 70
Tension: maintaining, 13; position of adjuster, 7
Thick and thin warps, 10, 15
Thrums, use of, 29
Tubing, 17
Twisting threads, 8, 9, 15

U
Uneven sheds, exploiting, 1, 55

W
Waistcoats, 16, 70, 71
Warping, 6–8
Warp patterns, 9–10
Waste, use of, 28, 29, 49
Wefts, floating, 61–2; insertions, 60–1; supplementary, 59–60; thick and thin, 61–2
Windows, wrapped, 31–3
Woven bands, interlacing of, 67
Wrapped warps, 31–4